from TOTEM POLES *to* TRILITHONS

THE STORY OF STONEHENGE FOR CHILDREN

by Romy Wyeth. Illustrations by Brian Lewis

Copyright © Romy Wyeth, May 1997
Copyright © Illustrations, Brian Lewis 1997

First published 1997 by Gemini

Gemini, Chitterne Road, Codford, Wiltshire BA12 0PG

All rights reserved. No part of this publication may be reproduced, copied or transmitted in any form or by any means, electronic, mechanical, photocopying, recording or otherwise, without the prior written permission of the publisher or in accordance with the Copyright Design and Patents Act 1988.

Typeset and designed by Southgate Publishers Ltd, Exmouth, Devon

Printed and bound in Great Britain by Short Run Press, Exeter, Devon

British Library Cataloguing in Publication Data
A CIP catalogue record for this book is available from the British Library.

ISBN 0 9515199 3 X

This book is dedicated to Megan, Emma and Henry, for when they are old enough to understand, to Laura, Emily, Jessica and Matthew, my first readers, whose encouragement and comments were invaluable, and to children everywhere, in the hope that they will recognize the magic!

CONTENTS

The People at the Dawn of Time	5
The Mysterious Landscape	9
Bluestones and Beakers	10
Arrival of the Stranger Stones	12
The Sarsen Circle	18
The Devil's Stone	19
A Prehistoric Puzzle	20
The Druid Priesthood	20
Stonehenge Completed	22
The Mother Goddess	23
The Enigma of the Plain	24
The Giants' Dance	25
Merlin's Monument	25
Time Travellers	26
Earth Magic – Dragon Power	27
The Airfields of the First World War	28
Mr Chubb Buys the Stones	29
The Military and the Plain	29
A Wonder of the World	32

THE PEOPLE AT THE DAWN OF TIME

Building the henge bank

ABOUT five thousand years ago, at the very dawn of time for mankind, the first settlers came to the area of chalk downland which we now call Salisbury Plain. They had ceased to be nomadic hunters and gatherers, wandering across the vast landscape following wild game. Instead they were the early farmers, gathering together in settlements, planting crops and domesticating animals.

It was at this time, in the New Stone Age, that the building of what has become known as Stonehenge was started. Three thousand years before Jesus was born, these early farmers built a huge circular bank of chalk, more than 2 metres high, with an opening in the direction of the sunrise.

At about the same time that the earthwork bank, which was called a "henge", was built, the people dug a series of 56 pits in a circle inside the bank. Today these pits are called the "Aubrey Holes" after the man who found them, John Aubrey.

During the Civil War in England, which was fought between 1642 and 1651, the forces of King Charles I and of Parliament were in conflict because they disagreed as to how the country should be governed. The soldiers of Parliament's army were known as the Roundheads because of the shape of their helmets, and the King's supporters were called Royalists or Cavaliers. King Charles I was beheaded on 30th January 1649 outside Whitehall Palace in London. His son, later to become King Charles II, continued to fight for another two years, until the final bloody battle at Worcester in 1651, when he was forced to flee for his life. The Roundheads had won and the Royalists were in retreat.

Charles had many adventures before he reached safety. Because he was very dark skinned and nearly 2 metres tall he was hard to disguise. The wanted posters described him as "a black man

King Charles at Stonehenge

two yards high"! (A yard is about the same as a metre.) At one time Charles hid in the branches of a huge oak tree, hidden by the thick leaves, while the Roundhead army searched below.

On his way to the south coast, where he escaped by boat to Europe, King Charles had hidden at Heale House in the Woodford Valley, just outside of the medieval city of Salisbury. During the day he left the house so that the servants would not know he was there. He rode his horse on to Salisbury Plain and while there he saw Stonehenge. When he returned to England in 1660, after nine years in exile, he asked John Aubrey to survey Stonehenge and Avebury in Wiltshire, another ancient site.

Some of the Aubrey Holes contained cremated human remains. The bodies had been burned and the ashes put in the holes. At this time the area may have been a cremation cemetery. However, this was not the main reason why the holes were dug, it would not have been a practical way of disposing of bodies. It is possible that the cremations were a form of ancestor worship, when people brought their dead families to the new religious site, perhaps as dedicatory burials.

Archaeologists are people who study the distant past, known as prehistory, which is the time before the Roman invasion of Britain 43 years after the birth of Jesus. In 1996 they discovered evidence that the Aubrey Holes were designed to hold large timbered posts, which were later removed. Some of the posts may have been burned. The holes may have been used for some kind of ritual or ceremony, but unless we really learn how to travel back in time, we shall never know for certain.

One idea about the purpose of the Aubrey Holes is connected with astronomy, the study of the heavens. Fifty-six is a number which divides well into calculations of the movements of the sun, the moon and the planets. The moon waxes and wanes twice in 56 nights. The suggestion is that the priests and wise men of the early farmers stood in the centre of the earthwork circle and counted the movements in the heavens of the sun, the moon and the planets over the bank which made a false horizon. They then used the pits as counting points to work out a calendar of the seasons, in the same way that the numbers on the face of a watch divide up a day. The farmers needed to know when to plant and harvest their crops and the most convenient time for their animals to give birth so as to ensure that the babies arrived in the springtime when the weather was mild and the grass was plentiful.

Archaeologists are people who study the past.

Just outside the opening in the bank, the ancient people were doing other calculations. Post holes have been found and these show that poles were put in to line up with the moon at various points on the horizon. These holes represent six lunar or moon years of observations five thousand years ago. As each lunar year is the same as 18.61 of our earth years, this means that for 111 years, the Neolithic (or New Stone Age) people were watching, counting and marking the sun, the moon and the planets as they orbited the night sky.

Other post holes found to the north of the monument, in what today is the car park, are now thought to date from the late ninth and early eighth millennium before Christ. A millennium is a period of a thousand years, so more than ten thousand years ago, in what is known as the Early Mesolithic or Middle Stone Age period, enormous pine posts were placed in these holes.

At this time the people were known as hunter-gatherers. They had yet to learn how to tame the wild animals and gather seeds to plant so that they could settle in one place and not starve. In order to survive they were forced to travel across the country following herds of wild game, fish and wildfowl, and to journey to places where food grew. In the forests that covered much of the land these tribes hunted deer, wild ox and boar with bows and arrows. It is likely that each tribe had a totem pole to represent their clan, and that these would have been carved with images of their gods or of wild animals and birds. The car park post holes may have been where the totem poles were placed when the tribe were on the Plain.

In order for the totem poles to have had any impact they would need to have been sited in an area where there were no trees. The Salisbury Plain landscape was thickly covered with pine and hazel trees at this time, but it is likely that the hunter-gatherers cleared large open areas amid the trees to encourage wild animals to feed and to make it easier for successful hunting.

Some astronomers have suggested that the car park post holes were placed to align with various sun and moon rising and setting points on the horizon.

About a hundred years after the henge bank was built, the first of a series of wooden structures was erected in the centre. These structures may have been sacred buildings.

Each tribe had a totem pole.

from TOTEM POLES *to* TRILITHONS

THE MYSTERIOUS LANDSCAPE

AROUND the site other mysterious mounds were built. Across from the entrance a double bank, over 2 miles (3 kilometres) long, was built from horizon to horizon. Today we call it the Greater Cursus. When it was first discovered in recent history, about three hundred years ago, people believed that Stonehenge was a Roman temple, left over from the Roman occupation of Britain that began in AD43 and lasted for four centuries. They assumed that the cursus was used by the Romans as a race track for their chariots.

What purpose the cursus served is lost in the mists of time. Was it for mystical ceremonies or had it a more practical use? Maybe it was built because ancient man saw what he believed was the marriage of the Sky God and the Earth Goddess. Perhaps, some time in prehistory, a funnel of air, like a small

Birds would clean the flesh ...

tornado, tore up the earth and trees, and the people of the Plain believed that this signified a union of their gods and built the cursus banks to commemorate the sacred marriage. At this time also we know that a man of great importance died on Salisbury Plain.

After death, the most revered people were placed in great earth mounds, called "long barrows". First their bodies were laid on high wooden platforms, safe from the animals, so that the birds could clean all the flesh from the bones. They were then laid in wooden or stone mortuary or death houses. When they had enough skeletons of important people, the tribe would build a huge mound of earth, a long barrow, over them.

Even if there were as many as forty skeletons in the long barrow, all of them would be at the eastern end of the mound, in the direction of the sunrise. The barrows must have had ceremonial or religious importance, rather than a practical use, because they did not need to be of that length to take the bodies. Where today the main road between London and the West Country meets another at a crossroads, an enormous long barrow was built for just one very old man. Was he a chief or a priest or a builder of one of the earthwork monuments? We shall never know. Later the bodies of a man, a woman and four children were added to the burial mound.

When the henge, the cursus and the barrow were new, they were probably kept clear of all grass and vegetation. They would have been gleaming white chalk banks and mounds, standing out clearly against the vast green landscape.

BLUESTONES AND BEAKERS

AROUND 2400 BC the first of the two special types of stone appeared on the Plain. These were the Bluestones. Each stone weighed up to 4 tonnes and they were brought by the Beaker people from ten different sources within a small area of a few kilometres in the Preseli Mountains in South Wales. The Beaker people were named because of their distinctive pottery and burials. The body was buried in a crouched position in the earth and a pottery cup or "beaker" was placed beside it.

These people were in recorded time only for the period between the end of the

Long barrow during construction

The body was in a crouched position in the earth with a pottery cup or beaker beside it.

The epic river raft journey of the Bluestones

New Stone Age and the beginning of the Bronze Age, from about 2400 BC until 1550 BC, the stone-building phase at Stonehenge. The Beaker people were great travellers and interested in mining and precious metals. It is possible that they found the Bluestones as they journeyed through the Welsh valleys on the way to the coast and Ireland, across the water. If it had been raining, as it does so often in the west, the sunlight hitting these stones would have made them look shining blue and perhaps magical beneath the lowering grey skies. This might explain why the Beaker people brought the stones from a distance of 130 miles (over 200 kilometres) as the crow flies.

The journey of the Bluestones was an epic one, beginning in South Wales and ending on the great Plain. They were transported 240 miles (almost 400 kilometres) by water, on rafts or dug-outs. Between the rivers the Bluestones would have been pulled overland. They were brought up the Bristol Channel, along the rivers of southern England to the meadows where five rivers meet (where in the thirteenth century the city of Salisbury was to be built) and then along the Wiltshire Avon to the area which today we call West Amesbury.

It was once believed that perhaps the Bluestones arrived naturally during the last Ice Age when the glaciers covering Britain melted. But even if the glaciers had travelled as far as the Plain, they would have brought other foreign stones and gravels on to the Plain, and there is no evidence of this. It was by men's endeavours and not nature's that the Bluestones came to the site so far from the Welsh mountains.

The Beaker people never finished the first phase of their building. They dug a double circle of holes to put the unworked stones in, but only put up three-quarters of them, in a pattern like a giant flattened arc. Shortly afterwards the stones were taken down, laid aside and not used again until many hundreds of years later when the Sarsen stones were in place. Some time during the Beaker period of history, before the arrival of the Bluestones, a young archer, about 180 centimetres tall, was killed. He was found in 1978, buried without ceremony in the ditch with two arrowheads embedded in his back, near where the first Bluestone arrangement was to be built. Maybe he was murdered and then hidden in the sacred enclosure, to be unearthed more than four thousand years later.

ARRIVAL OF THE STRANGER STONES

JESUS CHRIST is halfway between us and the latest date when the builders brought the Sarsen stones to Stonehenge more than four thousand years ago. The Sarsens arrived between 2400 and 2000 BC, possibly about 150 years after the Bluestones. The Beaker people were the first builders of the stone phase of Stonehenge, but by 2000 BC powerful tribes known as the Wessex Chieftains had arrived in the area with enormous flocks of sheep and herds of cattle, and they may have been responsible for the final setting of the stones.

The wheel had not yet been discovered when the huge sandstones were brought from the Marlborough Downs, 20 miles (30 kilometres) away to the north. The stones had to be pulled on enormous sleds or rollers made of tree trunks. If this was done in the winter, with ice on the ground, then moving the stones may have taken less effort as the sleds would slide on the frozen earth. Another possibility is that rails of wood were built across the Plain, and these rails could have been greased with animal fat to allow the stones to pass along them more easily.

The stones were pulled either by oxen or by men, and it has been estimated that it would have taken 1,000 men seven weeks in man hours to bring one of the 45-tonne stones to where we see them today. As the men would need to stop and rest, and so would possibly work only half a day, and as there were more than eighty Sarsen stones in the building, it was twenty years' work for a thousand men just to transport the stones.

The ancient people were building a very special place. Inside the earthwork bank of the early henge, they began their mammoth task.

The Sarsen stones got their name in medieval times. They were called after the Saracens, because they were foreign to the area. The Saracens were the strangers in the Holy Land where, in the Middle Ages, warriors went on Crusades, so the Sarsen stones were "the stranger stones". These were the days when Robin Hood roamed Sherwood Forest, the days when Richard I was king. He was known as Richard the Lionheart because of his bravery in battle. He was England's great Crusader king at a time when the European Christians were fighting the Arab Muslims over the holy places of both religions. Richard was in love with soldiering and warfare and spent only a

The Sarsen stones were pulled either by oxen or by men.

ARRIVAL OF THE STRANGER STONES

Mauls, some as small as tennis balls, some as big as boulders

few months in England in the ten years of his reign. He met his death in AD 1199, when he was just 41 years old, shot by an archer in the Limousin region of France.

The Sarsen stones are sandstone of a type that is very hard to shape. These stones are harder than steel and only a little less hard than diamonds. The only tool the builders could use to make any impact on the stones was Sarsen stone itself. Pieces of stone were made into round hammer stones or mauls, some were as small as a tennis ball, some the size of huge boulders.

Only a very few stones at the outside were not worked. The builders would have roughly shaped the stones where they found them so as to move as little weight as possible, then finished the work where the building was to be. The smooth, shaped stones had their best sides facing the inside, because this was where the ceremonies took place.

More than four thousand years ago, at the beginning of the time known as the Bronze Age, the Plain was half open landscape and the other half was heavily wooded. The people had lots of timber

from TOTEM POLES *to* TRILITHONS

to help them build. They used red deer antlers as picks to dig pits of between 120 and 180 centimetres deep in the chalk. Some of the pieces of these antlers can be found today. The builders carried away the surplus earth in the shoulder-blade bones of cattle and in woven baskets. Then, using wooden poles as levers, tied with ropes made of woven reeds or plant stems or animal hide, large teams of men moved the stones until they tipped into the pits in the chalk. They then packed stones loosely into the ground with the hammer stones they had been using.

To get the lintels or top stones into place they may have put pieces of wood under each end of the 6-tonne stone and then built a wooden platform underneath. Then they would lever the stones up, put more wood underneath and add to the wooden platform, eventually reaching the top of the upright stones and pushing the top stones across.

Another way they could have got the stones on top would have been to build ramps of wood and pull the stones up them. Ramps were sometimes made of earth but these were much more effort to make than the lighter, more portable and easily available wood. The earth would have to be constantly moved, a labour-intensive task which would leave traces that archaeologists could detect today.

By rubbing stone against stone, discarding dust specks, the builders carved joints in the stone. On the top of the upright stones they made huge tenons, which look like giant policemen's helmets, and under the top or lintel stones, they carved out enormous holes to fit the tenons in. Their earlier buildings were of wood, and they used the methods they had learned in carpentry to make their great stone temple.

Sarsen stones hoisted into place and lintels raised on huge wooden platforms

ARRIVAL OF THE STRANGER STONES

8000 BC

THE STONEHENGE TIMESCAPE

TEN THOUSAND YEARS OF HISTORY *1997*

THE SARSEN CIRCLE

FOUR thousand years ago, when the human world was still in its infancy, an enormous circle of 30 stones dominated the Plain. On top of the circle were 30 top stones, all touching and joined together with tongue-and-groove joints. One side of the stone had a piece sticking out and the other side a groove for another stone to fit in, just like a prehistoric jigsaw puzzle.

Inside the stone circle, the builders erected five great doorways, known as Trilithons because there were three stones in each. The five Trilithons were in the shape of a horseshoe or a bull's horn. They were smaller at the open end of the horseshoe, with the biggest Trilithon in the middle.

Perhaps the number of Trilithons had some significance. They may have represented the five planets that can still be seen in the night sky with the naked eye – Mercury, Venus, Mars, Jupiter and Saturn.

There were four stones outside the stone circle, these are called the Station Stones. These stones were not smoothed as the other stones had been. There were at least two pairs of entrance stones, and if you visit Stonehenge today you can see one of each of these stones leading into the monument.

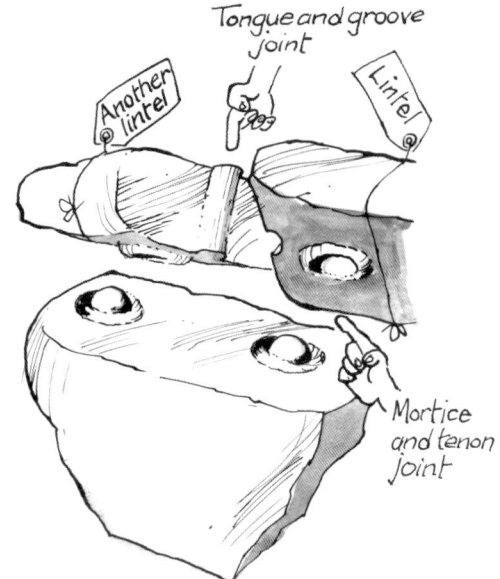

Joints were used to fit the stones together

Great doorways known as Trilithons stood inside the stone circle.

18   *from* TOTEM POLES *to* TRILITHONS

THE DEVIL'S STONE

THE first of these stones is called the Heel Stone, it weights 35 tonnes and it leans in towards the inner circle. There is a legend about this stone. Once upon a time, a very long time ago, the Devil decided he wished to puzzle and amaze mankind throughout eternity. He was in Ireland, and he saw an old lady whose garden was filled with enormous stones. The Devil offered to pay the old lady as much money as she could count while he moved the stones. The old lady thought that this would take the Devil a long time and that it would make her very rich. However, no sooner had she agreed and begun to count the coins, than the Devil had the stones on his shoulder and was away to Salisbury Plain.

On his way he dropped one of the stones in the River Avon, but all the rest he placed in the centre of the Plain. He was delighted with his success, convinced that he would confound the generations

The devil threw the stone at the friar with all his might.

to come as to where the stones came from and how they got there.

Passing by was a friar, and when he saw the Devil the holy man not unnaturally took to his heels. The Devil, realizing that someone knew the truth, picked up one of the enormous Sarsen stones and threw it at the fleeing man with all his might. The stone hit the friar on the foot, and the friar's heel mark can be seen on the stone to this very day.

The Heel Stone is also known as the Sun Stone. In the stories of ancient Greece there is a tale of an island far away in the west on which there is a great temple dedicated to the sun god, Apollo. The Greek word *hlios* means "sun".

It is a popular belief that the sunrise on the longest day of the year is directly over the Hlios, Hele or Heel Stone. This day, 21st June, is known as the Summer Solstice, the day when the sun seems to stand still in the sky. But the sunrise on this day was never directly over the Heel Stone from the centre of Stonehenge. The earth's position in the heavens was slightly different when the temple was being built, and the sun rose further to the west, between a pair of Heel Stones. The stones were part of the entrance to the ceremonial way into the building. It will not be until the year 3260, in twelve centuries' time, that the sun will rise over the Heel Stone from the centre of Stonehenge.

A PREHISTORIC PUZZLE

THE other entrance stone still to be seen has a very bloodthirsty name, the Slaughter Stone. In the seventeenth century travellers from far afield began to visit the ancient site. They saw how perfectly the stones were shaped and they were puzzled, just as the Devil would have wanted, by how the stones arrived and who brought them there.

The Celtic tribes who inhabited Britain before the Romans came found the great stone circle left by the Beaker people and imagined that the stones had been erected by a race of giants.

Forty-three years after Jesus was born, the Emperor Claudius had sent Roman legions from Italy to conquer Britain. The Romans occupied Britain for more than four hundred years, building a system of straight roads across the country which are still in use today. The roads were built by the legionary (soldier) engineers for the military. A legion was made up of 6,000 men, divided into units called Centuries, led by a Centurion. Each foot soldier was armed with a javelin and a double-edged sword. When they left, the period known as the Dark Ages began – this was the time of King Arthur and the Knights of the Round Table, according to legend.

The learned men of the seventeenth century at first decided that the Romans must have built Stonehenge. Later they discovered that when the Romans arrived, Stonehenge was already old and abandoned. So they thought about the earliest people in Britain who were able to build a place of such mystery, and they decided that Stonehenge must have been a Druid temple.

The Slaughter Stone, lying flat and with reddish stains from iron ore, looked like a blood-stained sacrificial stone. For centuries, even up to today there are people who believe that Druid priests sacrificed their victims by slitting their throats or cutting out their hearts on the stone. In fact this stone was another one of either two or three entrance stones into the site.

THE DRUID PRIESTHOOD

THE Druids were the earliest wise men in our history. They arrived here a thousand years after Stonehenge was abandoned, but probably never worshipped there because Stonehenge was a building and the Druids liked to worship in the open, in groves of trees, and near running water. The nearest water is 3 miles (nearly 5 kilometres) away from Stonehenge.

The Druids were a caste, which means that people were born Druids rather than deciding to become a member of the religion. Both men and women were Druids. They were the healers, the wise ones, the historians, the genealogists, the story-tellers, the priests, the judges, the poets and the magicians of the prehistoric peoples.

Nothing was written down, so all their knowledge had to be remembered and then passed on by word of mouth. The

Druids would retire into the forests or into deep caves, where they would study the lore of their ancestors. It has been said that it would have taken 20 years to accumulate all the knowledge they needed, and that this was in the form of verse.

The Druids knew about astronomy, and the fact that the lunar, or moon, year took almost 19 years to complete its cycle. They understood calendars, they used fire and water in their mystical ceremonies, and ritual weapons for human and animal sacrifice to their gods.

The Druids were the leaders in a well-ordered society, so when the Romans arrived the Druids were the focus for resistance to the invaders. As a result, the Romans systematically killed off the Druids until eventually none remained. This meant that all the knowledge which had passed from generation to generation for over five hundred years was lost. The Druids had written nothing down, everything was recorded in living memory, so the accumulated knowledge of generations disappeared from the earth for ever.

Stonehenge was a ruin before the invading Romans destroyed the Druids.

THE DRUID PRIESTHOOD

STONEHENGE COMPLETED

BY 1600 BC Stonehenge was finished. The Bluestones had been reintroduced and arranged in a circle inside the Sarsen Circle, with a horseshoe of 19 Bluestones inside the Trilithon horseshoe. Finally a very special stone was added. This stone came from Pembrokeshire in Wales and it is called the Altar Stone today. It is a micaceous sandstone, standing on the main axis, the line that goes exactly through the centre of Stonehenge. Today the Altar Stone is beneath the fallen lintel of the largest Trilithon, but it would have been upright at the very heart of the sanctuary when the building was finished. At different times it was possibly known as the Goddess Stone or the Stone at the Centre of the Known World

Perhaps on the longest day of the year, the Summer Solstice, the sun's first rays shone through the ceremonial entrance and touched the Goddess Stone, sym-

The central and greatest trilithon framing the midwinter sunset

bolizing the marriage of the Sky God and the Earth Goddess at midsummer.

Towards the end of all the efforts to complete the building – the earliest example of a building in the history of the world that we can still see today – the Processional Avenue was constructed. This comprised two parallel earthwork banks stretching from the river to the entrance of Stonehenge. Originally this may have been the route along which the Bluestones were brought to the site, following the contours of the land. Later perhaps it was the way the people came for their ceremonials, entering from the direction of the sunrise between several pairs of entrance stones.

The very final act in the building was a double circle of holes, known as the X and Y holes, dug between 1700 and 1500 BC. They were never used, but remained unfilled and their purpose is still a mystery.

By 1500 BC all the evidence of activity on the site stops. The people who had laboured for generations to build the great monument suddenly abandoned their sacred landscape. Their motivation for deserting the site must have been very compelling. Perhaps, fearing starvation, they were forced to move on to find fresh grazing for their livestock. Maybe a great plague came to the Plain and they died in large numbers, or it is possible that invaders came from across the sea and the people were wiped out in the bloodletting which followed.

So the grasses grew over the site, the earthwork banks became eroded and began to disappear as the wind and the rain beat across the exposed grassland. Beneath the darkening skies the seasons changed. The earth continued to turn, with no observers charting its progress. The henge and the great stone circle were forgotten.

THE MOTHER GODDESS

TO the people who live close to nature, the earth is a living being, a mother figure, caring for her people, feeding and providing for them. Unless the crops grew and the animals were plentiful, the people went hungry – they would starve, become sick and die. To the people of prehistory Mother Earth was sacred. One of the stones at Stonehenge has a carving said to be of a goddess from four thousand years ago.

People entered from the direction of the sunrise.

On death, people re-entered the womb of the earth which had given them life and sustained them. To some the burial mounds represented the womb of the Mother Goddess. The bodies were often in the position of a baby before birth, possibly because the people expected to be reborn in the future.

When the Christian Church was being established in Britain the old ways were still being practised. The pagan religion was nature-oriented, and it accepted an Earth Goddess. The priests wished to convert the pagan people to Christianity, so they built churches on the sites of ancient worship. This meant that in order to get to the old gods the people were forced into the new buildings.

The Church also encouraged reverence for the Virgin Mary, and the Mother Goddess and the Mother of Christ gradually became intermingled and then absorbed in each other. So eventually the new religion prevailed and the Mother Goddess was no longer worshipped or even remembered on the Plain.

THE ENIGMA OF THE PLAIN

THE Bronze Age people had been building in stone for almost a thousand years, so their motives must have been powerful indeed. The efforts they made tell us that they must have had plenty of food, because they were able to spare time from the fields to work on the building as well as to feed the builders. Their economy was such that they could also provide shelter and clothing for those toiling on the site. They must also have had a long period of peace, or they could not have used manpower for a communal project that took so many generations. What did they use Stonehenge for?

The building was the jewel in the crown of a very special area, a Valley of the Kings of the ancient Britons. Burial mounds and other earthwork monuments surround the site, so it was clearly a sacred landscape.

We know who the people were who built the different stages, we know the timescale, we know where the stones came from, and can guess how they were erected. What Stonehenge was is a little bit harder to be certain of.

Because these people were farmers, the seasons would have been important to them. As the days darkened and the earth became cold, they would fear that the sun was dying and there would never be warmth or light again. After the midwinter festival on the shortest day, the earth would begin to revive, plants and crops would grow and the life cycle would once again continue. When the people entered Stonehenge through the Ceremonial Way they faced the central and the greatest Trilithon. It framed the midwinter sunset, symbolising the reincarnation line of the earth.

From the site the sky arcs like the dome of an observatory, the heavens are cradled by the henge bank. Although the monument was possibly used as both a calendar and an observatory, if this was all they had been building the people had no need to go to so much trouble. All they needed were the four Station Stones and the Aubrey Holes and they could then chart all the important changing seasons of the year. The building was probably also used as a gathering place for important tribal rites – the swearing in of a new chief, the signing of a treaty, dynastic marriages, and so on.

Stonehenge was probably built with some religious or spiritual intention, a sacred place where worship was the prime purpose of all the efforts of countless generations.

THE GIANTS' DANCE

AS the world grew up, so too did the stories about Stonehenge. In the Middle Ages the people were very superstitious and they looked at the huge stone circle with awe and dread. They imagined that the stones were other people like themselves who had offended God in some way, perhaps by dancing on the sabbath day, and so they had been petrified, meaning "turned to stone", and doomed to dance across the Plain in an endless Giants' Dance throughout eternity.

MERLIN'S MONUMENT

MERLIN was the Druid magician in the legend of King Arthur and the Knights of the Round Table. In the fifth century after Christ, according to the story, Merlin moved the stones by magic to Salisbury Plain. They had come from Africa, but had been transported to Mount Killaraus in Ireland, where they were known as the "Giant's Round". These stones were believed to have healing powers. By washing in water which had been poured over the stones, a sick person would be cured.

At this time the high king of Britain was Vortigern the Thin, a Welsh noble of the Gewissei tribe who had achieved his position by treason. Threatened by his father-in-law, the Saxon King Hengist, Vortigern agreed to a meeting to prepare a peace treaty between the two factions on May Day at Amesbury. When they met, the Saxons pulled out hidden daggers from their boots and massacred

The Saxons pulled hidden daggers from their boots and massacred the British nobles.

TIME TRAVELLERS

IS it possible that, four thousand years ago, visitors from other planets arrived on earth in their spaceships? Maybe these aliens decided to build across the planet marvels that would astound earth people for generations – marvels such as the pyramids in Egypt and Mexico and the great stone circle at Stonehenge. Perhaps, as they revisited the earth throughout history, these time travellers used their monuments as sightlines to find their way from the vastness of space. Perhaps their spaceships are the UFOs (Unidentified Flying Objects) that have been seen across the world by countless people.

460 of the British nobles. It is said that the stones were transported by Merlin (some say by air, some by sea and some that the Devil brought them) and erected as a monument for these murdered Britons who were buried in a mass grave on the Plain.

Aurelius Ambrosius, the rightful king of Britain and King Arthur's uncle, later defeated Vortigern and reclaimed his throne. On his death he was buried in the Giant's Round, as was his brother, King Uther Pendragon, the father of King Arthur.

from TOTEM POLES *to* TRILITHONS

EARTH MAGIC – DRAGON POWER

Stonehenge has very powerful earth energy.

IMAGINE the earth as a living person, with veins of energy like the veins in the human body. These energy lines go all round the world, through the ancient sites. Although no one knows exactly what these lines are, by using rods of wood or metal or plastic, most people are able to detect their presence. The rods will cross on an energy line and uncross when the line has gone. The energy comes through our bodies, using them as conductors, then into the "dowsing" rods, as they are called.

Stonehenge has very powerful earth energy, earth forces or earth magic – it doesn't matter what you call it. The ancient Chinese talked of the Dragon Power in the distant past, long before Jesus was born, and called the energy lines the Dragon Paths. One of the legends of Stonehenge says it was a place of dragon or serpent worship; when you find a place associated with dragons or serpents in the past, these places have strong earth energy. Today we call them "ley lines".

Perhaps because prehistoric people were so in tune with the earth, they could sense the earth's powers and they may have known how to harness and use them. So when they chose sacred places, for their temples or to bury their dead, they chose to build on sites where the earth force was strong. The people of the past were very close to nature, their whole lives depended upon the natural cycle and the changing seasons. One theory is that if a stone circle is placed on an earth energy point it will focus the energy with great potency, and Stonehenge is a very powerful place.

THE AIRFIELDS OF THE FIRST WORLD WAR

A Nieuport monoplane

SALISBURY Plain was where the first army airfield was built in 1910, at Larkhill, or the Hill of the Larks, not far from Stonehenge. The Royal Flying Corps was formed in 1912 and in that same year, on 5th July, the very first fatal crash occurred, when two young men testing an aeroplane crashed in a field and were killed.

Captain Eustace Lorraine was a Grenadier Guard who was stationed at Larkhill with No. 3 Squadron. He was flying with Staff Sergeant Richard Wilson of the Royal Engineers in a Nieuport monoplane, a plane with one engine. Earlier, Captain Lorraine had returned to the airfield in the Nieuport because he had lost height after the plane engine had misfired.

Staff Sergeant Wilson had tested the engine, and at 5.30 pm the two men took the aeroplane up again. While in the middle of a steep left-handed turn over Fargo Bottom the Nieuport nose-dived into the ground. Other aviators, who saw the crash, leapt into their motor cars and found that both men were alive, but seriously injured. A horse-drawn ambulance took the men to Bulford hospital, but sadly they died.

Airman's Cross was erected a year after the crash. It is made of Cornish granite and represents an aeroplane propeller. It was placed as a memorial by the young men's comrades and is at the intersection of four roads not far from Stonehenge.

There is an enduring story that during the First World War the military wanted to move Stonehenge because it was a danger to their low-flying aircraft! The camp at Larkhill sprawled across the prehistoric landscape as far as the cursus, the Stonehenge aerodrome appeared to the west of the monument, and there was even a Stonehenge branch line from the Larkhill to Winterbourne Stoke railway.

MR CHUBB BUYS THE STONES

ON 21st September 1915 "Lot 15. Stonehenge with about 30 acres, 2 rods, 37 perches of adjoining downland" was sold at auction for £6,600 to Mr Cecil Chubb. The monument and the farmland around it had been part of the Amesbury Estate, sold when the heir died in action in the First World War, shortly followed by his father. Now it was the property of a local man who bought it on impulse. In 1918 Stonehenge was given to the nation by Cecil Chubb, and the Government gave the donor a knighthood.

Sir Cecil Chubb died, aged 58, in 1934, 19 years and a day after becoming the last man to own Stonehenge. He is buried in Roman Road Cemetery in Salisbury. Few people know that he was the national benefactor who secured the monument for the nation.

THE MILITARY AND THE PLAIN

THE chalk downland of the Plain, where once the nomadic hunters, the early farmers and the builders of Stonehenge roamed and worshipped, is today a vast military training ground and an agricultural landscape. The Army came to Salisbury Plain in 1872, claiming an area of 800 square miles (2,000 square kilometres). They wanted more space to establish safer artillery ranges after a young cadet was hit by a cannonball at Woolwich Common. No army wants to train young men to fight foreign wars and then accidentally shoot them themselves!

Around 1898 an agricultural decline began in Britain when the Government decided to buy grain from America and Canada. The Army purchased large tracts of this agricultural land to practise their cavalry charges. By the beginning of the twentieth century there were permanent camps at Bulford and Tidworth, while the testing and development of military aircraft at Upavon and Boscombe Down continues to the present day.

During the Second World War the Plain was an immense military camp, especially in 1943 and early 1944 as the build-up to the invasion of Europe began. This started with Operation Overlord and included the D-Day landings on the Normandy Beaches in France on 6th June 1944. The main nationalities to be found there were British, Americans, Canadians, French and Poles.

Today the military presence is still on Salisbury Plain. The camps and the airfields are in use and international exercises take place on a regular basis, such as training for the Gulf War of 1991 and the Bosnian conflict. The cavalry horses have now been replaced by tanks and jeeps. The sound of distant gunfire, like the far away thunder of a summer evening, can often be heard on days when the red flag is hoisted to warn of live firing on the Army ranges.

From prehistory to present-day military activities

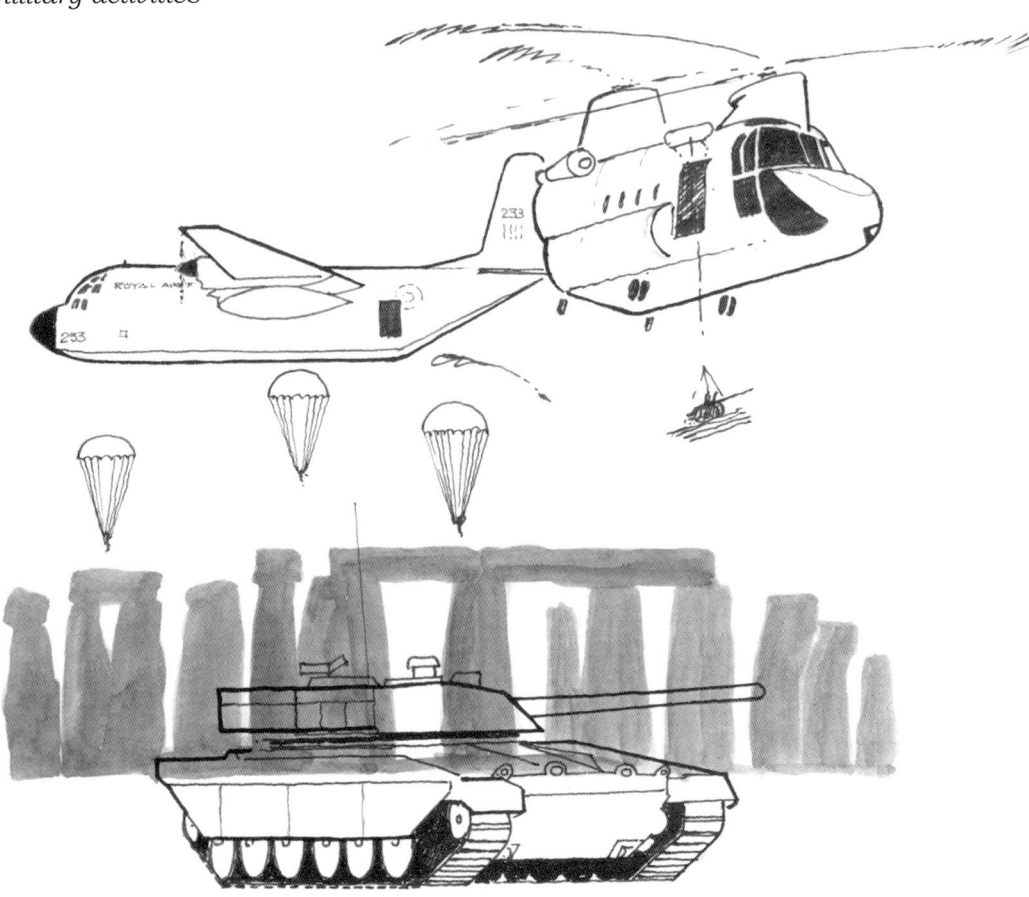

In place of the pioneer aviators in their monoplanes the skies are a backdrop for the huge Hercules aircraft, nicknamed "Fat Albert" because of its size, which parachute men and equipment on to the training areas. Chinook helicopters, with field guns in slings beneath them, circle the tree tops, and jet aircraft scream across the heavens, leaving feathery white trails across the blue expanse above the Plain and the great stone circle of Stonehenge.

What the military don't use for training is rented out to local farmers for agriculture. Cereal crops and hay are grown in abundance. The bright yellow of rape, used for oil or cattle feed, is followed by the blue of linseed or flax. Then, as the summer progresses, the scarlet poppy can be seen, a vivid wildflower that flourished from the beginning of time and garlanded the landscape before Stonehenge appeared in history. Cows and sheep graze the open fields just as they did four thousand years ago when the Beaker people were building the monument that has outlived civilizations.

from TOTEM POLES *to* TRILITHONS

A WONDER OF THE WORLD

FROM the totem poles of the hunter-gatherers to the trilithons of the Bronze Age builders, and now to the tourist buses of the twentieth century, Stonehenge remains a focal point for people of every faith and colour. It is the best-known monument on earth: every year millions of visitors from all across the world journey to Wiltshire to see the great stone circle. It is a wonder of the ancient world, a miracle of prehistoric engineering and a testament to the faith and vision of peoples who have long since disappeared from time.

Stonehenge is like a mirror, reflecting a vision of what each person looking at it expects to see. The temple from the dawn of history is a place of mystery, of magic and of enduring wonder.

from TOTEM POLES *to* TRILITHONS